EMPLOYEE RECEIPT

I acknowledge receipt of J. J. Keller's **Hazmat Made Easier Handbook** Second Edition, which covers 12 different hazmat topics. These topics include:

✓ **W9-BVL-257**

Hazmat Table (172.101)

Shipping Papers (Part 172, Subpart C)

Marking (Part 172, Subpart D)

Labeling (Part 172, Subpart E)

Placarding (Part 172, Subpart F)

Incident Reporting (171.15 & 171.16)

Emergency Response (172.602)

Training and Security (Part 172, Subparts H & I)

Loading/Unloading (Part 177, Subpart B)

Load Segregation (177.848)

Packaging (Part 178, Subpart L)

Definitions (171.8)

_____   _____

Employee's Signature   Date

_____

Company

_____

Company Supervisor's Signature

NOTE: This receipt shall be read and signed by the employee. A responsible company supervisor shall countersign the receipt and place it in the employee's training file.

REMOVABLE PAGE - PULL SLOWLY FROM TOP RIGHT CORNER

Hazmat
Made
Easier
Handbook

Second
Edition

J. J. Keller
& Associates, Inc.
Since 1953

©Copyright 2007

J. J. Keller & Associates, Inc.

3003 W. Breezewood Lane, P.O. Box 368

Neenah, Wisconsin 54957-0368

Phone: (920) 722-2848

www.jjkeller.com

Library of Congress Catalog Card Number: 2002108740

ISBN 1-59042-716-5

Canadian Goods and Services Tax (GST) Number: R123-317687

Printed in the U.S.A.

Second Edition, Third Printing, January 2007

Hazmat Made Easier

Table of Contents

Introduction

Whatever your role in the hazardous materials transportation process, Keller's *Hazmat Made Easier* is designed to help you better understand the hazmat regulations and what you have to do to meet the requirements.

Inside, you'll find 12 topics dealing with the various responsibilities people in the hazmat business must face every day: "The Hazardous Materials Table," "Documentation/Shipping Papers," "Marking," "Labeling," "Placarding," and more.

This handbook may not contain everything you need to become an expert in the hazmat transportation process. It will be an important tool you can use to become more familiar with the requirements and regulations the federal government has put in place to insure hazardous materials move safely across the United States.

Hazmat Made Easier will provide you with basic information to make certain you understand the responsibilities and requirements associated with your job, whether it is filling out shipping papers or placarding a truck loaded with hazardous materials.

Many times, in the hectic pace of a busy, work-filled day, it is either hard or just plain impossible to find a specific regulation that deals with a job function you have to perform. Sometimes you are simply on your own, with no one to help or guide you.

Topics in *Hazmat Made Easier* include reference to the Hazardous Materials Regulations that will specifically address the subject matter. That means when you need additional information on a topic, *Hazmat Made Easier* will help you find that particular regulation and get the word-for-word requirements fast.

We are sure this handbook will prove to be a valuable training tool to help you become more familiar with the Hazardous Materials Regulations, and a dependable source of reference throughout your hazmat career.

Hazmat Table
(172.101)

The Hazardous Materials Table lists materials that have been identified as hazardous by the U.S. Department of Transportation. The Table will provide you with most of the information you will need to prepare your hazmat shipment for transportation.

Classification (173.2)

Determining whether a material is hazardous is the first challenge you face in the hazmat transportation process. Once you have determined a material is hazardous, you can proceed to the Hazardous Materials Table and continue on in the process.

What exactly is a hazardous material?

49 CFR 171.8 defines a hazardous material as a material that is "capable of posing an unreasonable risk to health, safety, and property when transported in commerce." A material is considered "hazardous" if it meets one or more of the hazard class definitions in the hazmat regulations and/or is a hazardous substance, hazardous waste, marine pollutant, or elevated temperature material.

Hazmat Table

Nine hazard classes are listed in the hazmat regulations, and some of those classes are broken down into divisions, as well as a category known as "Other Regulated Material" or "ORM-D."

Class No.	Division No. (if any)	Name of class or division	49 CFR reference for definitions
None		Forbidden materials	173.21
None		Forbidden explosives	173.54
1	1.1	Explosives (with a mass explosion hazard)	173.50
1	1.2	Explosives (with a projection hazard)	173.50
1	1.3	Explosives (with predominantly a fire hazard)	173.50
1	1.4	Explosives (with no significant blast hazard)	173.50
1	1.5	Very insensitive explosives; blasting agents	173.50
1	1.6	Extremely insensitive detonating substances	173.50
2	2.1	Flammable gas	173.115
2	2.2	Non-flammable compressed gas	173.115
2	2.3	Poisonous gas	173.115
3		Flammable and combustible liquid	173.120
4	4.1	Flammable solid	173.124
4	4.2	Spontaneously combustible material	173.124
4	4.3	Dangerous when wet material	173.124
5	5.1	Oxidizer	173.127
5	5.2	Organic peroxide	173.128
6	6.1	Poisonous materials	173.132
6	6.2	Infectious substance (Etiologic agent)	173.134
7		Radioactive material	173.403
8		Corrosive material	173.136
9		Miscellaneous hazardous material	173.140
None		Other regulated material: ORM-D	173.144

If you run into a situation where the hazmat you are working with meets the definition of more than one hazard class, refer to 173.2a — *Classification of a material having more than one hazard.*

Using the Hazardous Materials Table (172.101)

The single, most important step in using the Hazardous Materials Table and beginning to prepare your shipment is to make sure you choose the correct proper shipping name. Once you have located it in the Table, you will be able to find the shipping information you need in the corresponding columns.

Column 1 — Symbols (172.101)

Column 1 has 6 symbols that are used to identify hazmat with special shipping instructions.

The 6 symbols are:

Symbol	Meaning
+	Fixes the proper shipping name, hazard class, and packing group without regard to whether the material meets the definition of that class or packing group, or meets any other hazard class definition.
A	Restricts the application of the requirements to materials offered for transportation by aircraft — unless the material is a hazardous substance or hazardous waste.
G	Identifies proper shipping names for which one or more technical names must be entered in parentheses, in association with the basic description.
D	Identifies proper shipping names which are appropriate for domestic transportation, but which may be inappropriate for international transportation.
I	Identifies proper shipping names which are appropriate for international transportation. An alternate proper shipping name may be selected when only domestic transportation is involved.
W	Restricts the application of the requirements to materials offered for transportation by vessel — unless the material is a hazardous substance or hazardous waste.

Column 2 — Hazmat descriptions and proper shipping names (172.101)

Column 2 lists the descriptions and proper shipping names that can be used to describe hazardous materials. It is important to remember that the proper shipping names are the ones shown in **Roman type**, not *italics*.

However, words and punctuation marks in *italics* may be used in addition to the proper shipping name. They are not required to be used in your proper shipping name description. It is your choice.

	Sample from the Hazardous Materials Table								
Symbols	Hazardous materials descriptions and proper shipping names	Hazard class or Division	Identification Numbers	PG	Label Codes	Special provisions (§172.102)	(8) Packaging (§173.***)		
							Exceptions	Non-bulk	Bulk
(1)	(2)	(3)	(4)	(5)	(6)	(7)	(8A)	(8B)	(8C)
	Pentachloroethane	6.1	UN1669	II	6.1	IB2, T7, TP2	153	202	243
	Pentachlorophenol	6.1	UN3155	II	6.1	IB8, IP2, IP4, T3, TP33	153	212	242
	Pentaerythrite tetranitrate (dry)	Forbidden							
	Pentaerythrite tetranitrate mixture, desensitized, solid, n.o.s. *with more than 10 percent but not more than 20 percent PETN, by mass*	4.1	UN3344	II	4.1	118, N85	None	214	None

What happens when you can't find the technical name of the hazmat in Column 2?

It is possible the material may not be hazardous. If it is, you must select a generic or n.o.s. name that most accurately describes the hazmat.

If a name has not already been picked or determined, it may be a good idea to talk with your supervisor/manager to make certain the right name is selected.

Column 3 — Hazard class or division (172.101)

Column 3 shows the hazard class or division that corresponds to the proper shipping name. Because the hazard class or division number will help determine how a hazmat is packaged and labeled, it is very important that the one listed for the selected proper shipping name matches the material being transported. This is especially true when more than one hazard class or division is shown.

Sample from the Hazardous Materials Table

Symbols	Hazardous materials descriptions and proper shipping names	Hazard class or Division	Identification Numbers	PG	Label Codes	Special provisions (§172.102)	(8) Packaging (§173.***)		
							Exceptions	Non-bulk	Bulk
(1)	(2)	(3)	(4)	(5)	(6)	(7)	(8A)	(8B)	(8C)
D G	Compounds, cleaning liquid	8	NA1760	I	8	A7, B10, T14, TP2, TP27	None	201	243
				II	8	B2, IB2, N37, T11, TP2, TP27	154	202	242
				III	8	IB3, N37, T7, TP1, TP28	154	203	241
D G	Compounds, cleaning liquid	3	NA1993	I	3	T11, TP1	150	201	243
				II	3	IB2, T7, TP1, TP8, TP28	150	202	242
				III	3	B1, B52, IB3, T4, TP1, TP29	150	203	242

The word "Forbidden" will be located in Column 3 when the hazmat in question is too hazardous to be transported. Keep in mind, however, that the prohibition may not apply if the hazmat is diluted or stabilized.

Column 4 — ID numbers (172.101)

Column 4 displays a proper shipping name's UN or NA identification number. Numbers preceded by "UN" mean the proper shipping name is appropriate for both domestic and international transportation, while numbers preceded by "NA" mean the proper shipping name is for domestic transportation only, as well as to and from Canada.

Sample from the Hazardous Materials Table

Symbols	Hazardous materials descriptions and proper shipping names	Hazard class or Division	Identification Numbers	PG	Label Codes	Special provisions (§172.102)	(8) Packaging (§173.***)		
							Exceptions	Non-bulk	Bulk
(1)	(2)	(3)	(4)	(5)	(6)	(7)	(8A)	(8B)	(8C)
D	Diesel fuel	3	NA1993	III	None	144, B1, IB3, T4, TP1, TP29	150	203	242
I	Diesel fuel	3	UN1202	III	3	144, B1, IB3, T2, TP1	150	203	242

Column 5 — Packing group (PG) (172.101)

Column 5 provides the PG number that corresponds to the proper shipping name and hazard class of the hazmat. The packing group tells you the degree of danger a hazmat presents during transportation.

Hazmat Table

If more than one packing group is shown for a proper shipping name, you will have to refer to the class-specific sections in Part 173 (173.121 for Class 3, 173.125 for Class 4, etc.), to determine the packing group for your material.

- **Packing Group I** indicates great danger.
- **Packing Group II** indicates medium danger.
- **Packing Group III** indicates minor danger.

You will notice that no PG number is assigned to Class 2, Class 7, ORM-D materials, and some Division 6.2 and Class 9 materials.

Sample from the Hazardous Materials Table

Symbols	Hazardous materials descriptions and proper shipping names	Hazard class or Division	Identification Numbers	PG	Label Codes	Special provisions (§172.102)	(8) Packaging (§173.***)		
							Exceptions	Non-bulk	Bulk
(1)	(2)	(3)	(4)	(5)	(6)	(7)	(8A)	(8B)	(8C)
	Engines, internal combustion, *flammable gas powered*	9	UN3166		9	135	220	220	220
	Engines, internal combustion, *flammable liquid powered*	9	UN3166		9	135	220	220	220
G	**Environmentally hazardous substances, liquid, n.o.s.**	9	UN3082	III	9	8, 146, IB3, T4, TP1, TP29	155	203	241

Column 6 — Labels (172.101)

Column 6 identifies the label codes that correspond with the hazard warning label(s) that must be applied to the hazmat's packaging, unless the material is excepted from the labeling requirements.

Sample from the Hazardous Materials Table

Symbols	Hazardous materials descriptions and proper shipping names	Hazard class or Division	Identification Numbers	PG	Label Codes	Special provisions (§172.102)	(8) Packaging (§173.***)		
							Exceptions	Non-bulk	Bulk
(1)	(2)	(3)	(4)	(5)	(6)	(7)	(8A)	(8B)	(8C)
	Carbon dioxide, refrigerated liquid	2.2	UN2187		2.2	T75, TP5	306	304	314, 315
A W	**Carbon dioxide, solid** *or* **Dry ice**	9	UN1845	III	None		217	217	240
	Carbon disulfide	3	UN1131	I	3, 6.1	B16, T14, TP2, TP7, TP13	None	201	243
	Carbon monoxide, compressed	2.3	UN1016		2.3, 2.1	4	None	302	314, 315
	Carbon monoxide and hydrogen mixture, compressed	2.3	UN2600		2.3, 2.1	6	None	302	302

What happens when more than one label code is listed?

The first code indicates the primary hazard; additional codes indicate subsidiary or secondary hazards. See the Labeling topic for additional information on primary and subsidiary hazards.

Column 7 — Special provisions (172.101)

Column 7 is where you will find special provisions that provide specific instructions about the hazmat. The codes in Column 7 are found in Section 172.102.

Sample from the Hazardous Materials Table									
Sym-bols	Hazardous materials descriptions and proper shipping names	Hazard class or Division	Identifica-tion Numbers	PG	Label Codes	Special provisions (§172.102)	(8) Packaging (§173.***)		
							Excep-tions	Non-bulk	Bulk
(1)	(2)	(3)	(4)	(5)	(6)	(7)	(8A)	(8B)	(8C)
	Borneol	4.1	UN1312	III	4.1	A1, IB8, IP3, T1, TP33	None	213	240
+	Boron tribromide	8	UN2692	I	8, 6.1	2, B9, B14, B32, B74, N34, T20, TP2, TP12, TP13, TP38, TP45	None	227	244
	Boron trichloride	2.3	UN1741		2.3, 8	3, B9, B14	None	304	314
	Boron trifluoride	2.3	UN1008		2.3	2, B9, B14	None	302	314, 315

A number listed by itself means it applies to multi-modal transportation; the various letters used and what they apply to are:

Code	Applies to
A	Transportation by aircraft
B	Bulk packagings, other than UN, IM specification portable tanks, or IBCs
IB or IP	Transportation in IBCs
N	Non-bulk packaging
R	Transportation by rail
T	Transportation in UN or IM specification portable tanks
TP	Additional UN or IM specification portable tank information, as required
W	Transportation by water

Column 8 — Packaging (172.101)

Column 8 is made up of three separate columns of packaging authorizations:

- **8A** is for exceptions.

- **8B** is for non-bulk packaging.

- **8C** is for bulk packaging.

If the word "None" is shown in any of the three columns, the exception or that type of packaging — non-bulk and/or bulk — is not authorized, except as may be provided in the Special provisions column.

								(8) Packaging (§173.***)	
Symbols	Hazardous materials descriptions and proper shipping names	Hazard class or Division	Identification Numbers	PG	Label Codes	Special provisions (§172.102)	Exceptions	Non-bulk	Bulk
(1)	(2)	(3)	(4)	(5)	(6)	(7)	(8A)	(8B)	(8C)
	Magnesium peroxide	5.1	UN1476	II	5.1	IB6, IP2, T3, TP33	152	212	242
	Magnesium phosphide	4.3	UN2011	I	4.3, 6.1	A19, N40	None	211	None
	Magnesium, powder or Magnesium alloys, powder	4.3	UN1418	I	4.3, 4.2	A19, B56	None	211	244
				II	4.3, 4.2	A19, B56, IB5, IP2, T3, TP33	None	212	241
				III	4.3, 4.2	A19, B56, IB8, IP4, T1, TP33	None	213	241

Sample from the Hazardous Materials Table

You'll notice that, at the top of Column 8, there is §173.*** in parentheses. The numbers listed in the three columns of Column 8 should be substituted for the three asterisks following 173.

For example, if 152 is listed in Column 8A, you would reference §173.152 for exceptions.

Column 9 — Quantity limitations (172.101)

Column 9 lists quantity limitations for passenger-carrying aircraft or rail cars in Column 9A, and cargo aircraft only in Column 9B. The quantities shown are the maximum quantities you can offer for transport in a **single** packaging.

Sample from the Hazardous Materials Table

Symbols	Hazardous materials descriptions and proper shipping names	Hazard class or Division	Identification Numbers	PG	Label Codes	Special provisions (§172.102)	(8) Packaging (§173.***)			(9) Quantity limitations	
							Exceptions	Non-bulk	Bulk	Passenger aircraft/rail	Cargo aircraft only
(1)	(2)	(3)	(4)	(5)	(6)	(7)	(8A)	(8B)	(8C)	(9A)	(9B)
	Sodium monoxide	8	UN1825	II	8	IB8, IP2, IP4, T3, TP33	154	212	240	15 kg	50 kg
	Sodium nitrate	5.1	UN1498	III	5.1	A1, A29, IB8, IP3, T1, TP33	152	213	240	25 kg	100 kg
	Sodium nitrate and potassium nitrate mixtures	5.1	UN1499	III	5.1	A1, A29, IB8, IP3, T1, TP33	152	213	240	25 kg	100 kg
	Sodium nitrite	5.1	UN1500	III	5.1, 6.1	A1, A29, IB8, IP3, T1, TP33	152	213	240	25 kg	100 kg
	Sodium pentachlorophenate	6.1	UN2567	II	6.1	IB8, IP2, IP4, T3, TP33	153	212	242	25 kg	100 kg

If you see the word "Forbidden," the hazmat may not be offered or transported in the mode listed.

Column 10 — Vessel stowage (172.101)

Column 10 lists the various authorized locations for hazmat stowage aboard a vessel. Column 10A specifies stowage locations on passenger and cargo vessels; Column 10B lists additional requirements for specific types of hazardous materials.

Sample from the Hazardous Materials Table

Symbols	Hazardous materials descriptions and proper shipping names	Hazard class or Division	Identification Numbers	PG	Label Codes	Special provisions (§172.102)	(8) Packaging (§173.***)			(10) Vessel stowage	
							Exceptions	Non-bulk	Bulk	Location	Other
(1)	(2)	(3)	(4)	(5)	(6)	(7)	(8A)	(8B)	(8C)	(10A)	(10B)
	Ferrosilicon, with 30 percent or more but less than 90 percent silicon	4.3	UN1408	III	4.3, 6.1	A1, A19, B6, IB8, IP4, IP7, T1, TP33	151	213	240	A	13, 40, 52, 53, 85, 103
	Ferrous arsenate	6.1	UN1608	II	6.1	IB8, IP2, IP4, T3, TP33	153	212	242	A	
D	Ferrous chloride, solid	8	NA1759	II	8	IB8, IP2, IP4, T3, TP33	154	212	240	A	
D	Ferrous chloride, solution	8	NA1760	II	8	B3, IB2, T11, TP2, TP27	154	202	242	B	40
	Ferrous metal borings or Ferrous metal shavings or Ferrous metal turnings or Ferrous metal cuttings in a form liable to self-heating	4.2	UN2793	III	4.2	A1, A19, IB8, IP3, IP7	None	213	241	A	
	Fertilizer ammoniating solution with free ammonia	2.2	UN1043		2.2		306	304	314, 315	E	40

Hazmat Table

The codes in 10A are:

Code	Meaning
A	The material may be stowed "on deck" or "under deck" on both passenger and cargo vessels.
B	A material may be stowed "on deck" or "under deck" on a cargo vessel and on a passenger vessel carrying a number of passengers limited to not more than the larger of 25 passengers, or one passenger per each three meters of overall vessel length. A material may be stowed "on deck only" on passenger vessels in which the number of passengers specified in the previous sentence is exceeded.
C	The material must be stowed "on deck only" on both cargo and passenger vessels.
D	A material must be stowed "on deck only" on a cargo vessel and on a passenger vessel carrying a number of passengers limited to not more than the larger of 25 passengers or one passenger per each three meters of overall vessel length. The material is prohibited on passenger vessels in which the limiting number of passengers in the previous sentence is exceeded.
E	A material may be stowed "on deck" or "under deck" on a cargo vessel and on a passenger vessel carrying a number of passengers limited to not more than the larger of 25 passengers, or one passenger per each three meters of overall vessel length. The material is prohibited from carriage on passenger vessels in which the limiting number of passengers in the previous sentence is exceeded.

The numerical codes in 10B are found in 176.84(b).

Notes

Notes

Shipping Papers
(Part 172, Subpart C)

Shipping papers serve a number of functions, such as providing key information about the hazmat being transported. Emergency response is one important thing to consider when you fill out a shipping paper. Someone's life may depend on it. What you put on the shipping paper could provide emergency responders the information needed to make the difference between life and death if an incident occurs.

Shipping papers are required for each and every hazmat shipment, for all modes of transportation, unless specifically excepted by the Hazardous Materials Regulations.

How can you tell if a hazmat is excepted from shipping papers?

Exceptions are authorized for any hazmat listed in the Hazardous Materials Table identified in Column 1 by an "A" or "W" unless it is:

- Offered or transported by air or water.

- A hazardous waste.

- A hazardous substance.

- A marine pollutant.

An ORM-D that is intended or offered for transport by air must have shipping papers.

Shipping Papers

In most cases, shipping papers must be prepared by the person who is offering the hazmat for transport. While the hazmat regulations do not specify what kind of a form you should use for shipping papers, the regulations are pretty specific about what information should be provided.

Here is an example of a typical form and the information needed:

Hazmat entries (172.201)

Hazmat entries must be easily identified on the shipping paper. If both hazardous and non-hazardous materials are listed on the same shipping paper, the hazmat entries must be:

- Entered first, or

- Identified with an "X" or "RQ," as appropriate, in a column that is designated "HM," or

- Entered in a contrasting color (hazmat entries may be highlighted only on shipping paper copies).

Hazmat description (172.202)

The hazmat you are offering or transporting must be described using the information contained in the Hazardous Materials Table. The information required for the shipping description must include:

- The proper shipping name.
- The hazard class or division number.
- The subsidiary hazard class or division number entered in parentheses.
- The UN or NA identification number.
- The packing group (PG), if any.
- The total quantity of the hazmat, by net or gross mass, capacity, or as otherwise appropriate.
- Number and type of packages (mandatory October 1, 2007).

The first five items listed above are a hazardous material's basic description; it must be entered on the shipping paper in one of two ways. The sequence shown above is one option; the alternate sequence is shown below.

HM-215I adopted a requirement that the shipping description of a hazmat must be indicated on a shipping paper in the following manner:

Identification number listed first, followed by the proper shipping name, hazard class, subsidiary hazard in parentheses, and packing group. For example, "UN2744, Cyclobutyl chloroformate, 6.1, (8, 3), PG II."

A six-year transition period to implement the requirement was authorized; mandatory compliance will begin January 1, 2013. Either sequence may be used until then.

The total quantity of the hazmat, may be entered either before, after, or both before and after the material's basic description. It must also indicate the appropriate unit of measure, which may be abbreviated (gal, lbs, kg, etc.).

For domestic shipments, primary and subsidiary hazard class or division names may be entered following the numerical hazard class or division, or following the basic description.

Total quantity is not required for empty hazmat packaging, cylinders of Class 2 hazmat and bulk packagings. However, some indication of total quantity for Class 2 cylinders and bulk packagings must be shown (10 cylinders or 1 cargo tank).

Abbreviations are not usually allowed in the proper shipping name, except for "ORM" (Other Regulated Material), and abbreviations that actually are part of the description in Column 2 of the Hazardous Materials Table (TNT, PCB).

Additional information

Additional information about the hazmat may be entered on the shipping paper, provided it is put after the basic description and is not inconsistent with the required description.

Technical names (172.202 & 172.203)

If the proper shipping name has the letter "G" in Column 1 of the Hazardous Materials Table, the technical name must be entered in parentheses along with the basic description. The word "contains" or "containing" may be used, as needed.

> **Example:** *Flammable liquids, n.o.s. (contains Xylene and Benzene), 3, UN 1993, II.*

Reportable quantity (172.203)

The letters "RQ" must be entered before or after the basic description if the hazmat is a hazardous substance. The letters "RQ" may be placed in the HM column instead of an "X."

No. of packages	Description of articles, special marks, and exceptions	Hazard Class	I.D. Number	Packing Group	Weight (subject to correction)
1	Drum, RQ, Mercury	8	UN2809	III	400 lbs.

Limited quantity (172.203)

Limited quantity materials must have the words "Limited Quantity" or the abbreviation "Ltd. Qty." following the basic description.

Poisonous materials (172.203)

The word "Poison" or "Toxic" must be included in the shipping description for a Division 6.1 PG I or II hazmat if the proper shipping name or hazard class entry doesn't tell you it is a poison.

The technical name must be entered in parentheses along with the basic description for a Division 6.1 PG I or II, or Division 2.3 hazmat, if the technical name that makes the material a 6.1 or 2.3 is not included in the proper shipping name.

The words "Poison-Inhalation Hazard" or "Toxic-Inhalation Hazard" followed by "Zone A," "Zone B," "Zone C," or "Zone D," for gases, or "Zone A" or "Zone B" for liquids must be entered on the shipping description for hazmat poisonous by inhalation (PIH).

The word "Poison" or "Toxic" or the phrase "Poison-Inhalation Hazard" or "Toxic Inhalation Hazard" need not be repeated if it already appears in the shipping description.

Marine pollutants (172.203)

The words "Marine Pollutant" must be included with the basic description for a marine pollutant when the proper shipping name does not tell you it is a marine pollutant.

No. of packages	Description of articles, special marks, and exceptions	Hazard Class	I.D. Number	Packing Group	Weight (subject to correction)
1	Drum, Cadmium Compounds, Marine Pollutant	6.1	UN2570	III	450 lbs.

Elevated temperature material (172.203)

The word "HOT" must be placed in front of the proper shipping name if the hazmat is an elevated temperature material.

Special permits (172.203)

"DOT-SP" followed by the appropriate special permit number must be entered on the shipping paper so it is clearly associated with the description of the hazmat with the special permit.

Emergency response telephone number (172.604)

Most shipping papers are required to have a telephone number listed that can be called in an emergency. It must be the number of the person offering the material for transportation or an agency that is capable of, and accepts responsibility for, providing detailed emergency response information about the hazardous material(s) on the shipping paper.

The number must be entered on the shipping paper immediately following the description of the hazmat or entered once on the shipping paper in a visible location, indicating it is for emergency response information, provided the number applies to each hazmat listed.

Emergency response telephone number requirements do not apply to limited quantities of hazmat offered for transportation and materials properly described under the following shipping names:

- Battery powered equipment
- Battery powered vehicle
- Carbon dioxide, solid
- Castor bean
- Castor flake

- Castor pomace
- Consumer commodity
- Dry ice
- Engines, internal combustion
- Fish meal, stabilized
- Fish scrap, stabilized
- Refrigerating machine
- Vehicle, flammable gas powered
- Vehicle, flammable liquid powered
- Wheelchair, electric

For emergency assistance involving hazmat, four agencies are listed in the 2004 Emergency Response Guidebook. The agencies all requested to be listed as providers of emergency response information and agreed to provide emergency response information to all callers. Each provides advice 24 hours a day, 7 days a week, for anyone requesting assistance at the scene of an incident.

Agencies and the telephone numbers listed are:

CHEMTREC, (800) 424-9300
CHEM-TEL, INC., (800) 255-3924
INFOTRAC, (800) 535-5053
3E COMPANY, (800) 451-8346

Upon receipt of a call of an incident, the agency contacted will provide immediate advice and contact the shipper for more detailed information, as well as request assistance at the scene, as necessary. Contact the various agencies for more information about fees and services provided.

Shipping Papers

If the number is that of the person offering the material for transportation, the number must be monitored at all times the hazmat is being transported. The person must be knowledgeable of the hazards and characteristics of the hazmat, and must have emergency response and incident mitigation information for the material, or have immediate access to someone who does.

Answering machines, beepers/pagers, and voice mail are not acceptable!

Shipper's certification (172.204)

The shipper's certification certifies that the hazmat has been prepared in accordance with the regulations. The certification must be printed manually or mechanically on the shipping paper.

Retention (172.201 & 177.817)

Shippers are required to retain a copy or electronic image of each hazmat shipping paper for two years after the material is accepted by the initial carrier. Carriers must retain the shipping paper copy for one year after the material is accepted. Each shipping paper must include the date of acceptance by the carrier.

Hazardous waste manifests must be retained for three years by the shipper, by the initial carrier, and each subsequent carrier for three years from the date the waste was accepted by the initial carrier.

Notes

Notes

Marking
(Part 172, Subpart D)

Markings play an important part in the hazmat transportation process because they provide information about the hazardous material inside a packaging, freight container, or transport vehicle.

Marking requirements apply to non-bulk and bulk packagings transported by rail, air, vessel, and highway. Markings are sometimes confused with labeling and placarding. Labels and placards communicate the hazard class or division of the hazardous material; markings provide additional and more specific information about the hazmat.

Specifications (172.304)

Markings must be durable, in English, and printed on or affixed to the surface of a package or on a label, tag, or sign. Markings must be:

- displayed on a background of sharply contrasting color (like black letters on a white box),

- not concealed or hidden by other labels or attachments, and

- located away from any other markings, like advertising or trademarks, that could reduce their effectiveness substantially.

Non-bulk markings (172.301)

Non-bulk packagings must be marked with:

- The proper shipping name.

- Technical names, if required.

Marking

- UN or NA identification numbers.

- The consignee's or consignor's name and address.

- A DOT-E or DOT-SP (exemption number, special permit number), if required.

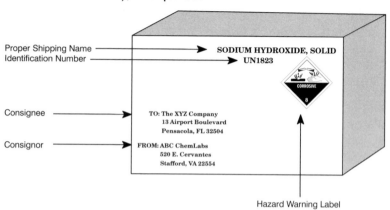

Proper Shipping Name — **SODIUM HYDROXIDE, SOLID**
Identification Number — **UN1823**

Consignee — TO: The XYZ Company
13 Airport Boulevard
Pensacola, FL 32504

Consignor — FROM: ABC ChemLabs
520 E. Cervantes
Stafford, VA 22554

Hazard Warning Label

Identification numbers are not required on non-bulk packages containing only limited quantities or ORM-D materials, except for limited quantities marked according to the requirements in 173.315.

The consignee's or consignor's name and address are not required if the non-bulk package is transported by highway only and will not be transferred from one motor carrier to another, or if it is transported as part of a carload lot, truckload lot, or freight container load, and the entire contents are shipped from one consignor to one consignee.

Large quantities of non-bulk packages (172.301)

A transport vehicle or freight container carrying a single hazmat in non-bulk packages must be marked on each side and each end with the hazmat's ID number, subject to the following:

- Each package is marked with the same proper shipping name and ID number;

- The aggregate gross weight of the hazmat is 4,000 kg (8,820 lb) or more;

- All of the hazmat is loaded at one loading facility; and

- The transport vehicle contains no other hazmat or non-hazardous material.

This requirement does not apply to Class 1 material, Class 7 material, or non-bulk packages that do not require identification numbers (such as limited quantities or ORM-D).

Poisonous hazmat (172.313)

A transport vehicle or freight container loaded at one loading facility with 1,000 kg (2,205 lb) or more of PIH material in Hazard Zone A or B in non-bulk packaging, all with the same shipping name and ID number, must be marked with the proper ID number on each side and each end.

If the transport vehicle or freight container has more than one PIH material that requires the markings just covered, the load must be marked with an ID number for only one of the hazardous materials. You determine the ID number by the following:

- The ID number of the hazmat having the greatest aggregate gross weight for different materials in the same hazard zone.

- The ID number of the hazmat for Hazard Zone A material when you have different materials in both Zone A and B.

Bulk markings (172.302)

Unless specifically excepted from the regulations, bulk packagings containing hazmat must be marked with the identification number specified in the Hazardous Materials Table for that material.

Marking

The identification number may be displayed on an orange panel, a placard, or on a white square-on-point configuration with the same outside dimensions as a placard.

The numbers must be marked on:

- Each side and each end if the packaging has a capacity of 3,785 L (1,000 gallons) or more.

- Two opposing sides if the packaging has a capacity less than 3,785 L (1,000 gallons).

- Each side and each end of a tube trailer motor vehicle with cylinders permanently installed.

Tanks (172.326 & 172.328)

Besides ID number markings, portable tanks containing a hazardous material must have the hazmat's proper shipping name legibly marked on two opposite sides, and the owner or lessee's name also displayed.

Except for certain nurse tanks, cargo tanks transporting Class 2 hazmat must be marked on each side and each end with the proper shipping name or appropriate common name of the gas.

A transport vehicle or freight container must be marked with ID numbers on each side and each end if the markings displayed on a portable tank or cargo tank transported on or in the transport vehicle or freight container are not visible.

A permanently installed cargo tank inside an enclosed cargo body of a transport vehicle or freight container is required to have the ID numbers displayed only on each side and end of the tank that are visible when the cargo tank is accessed.

NON-ODORIZED marking (172.301, 172.326, 172.328 & 172.330)

After September 30, 2006, no person may offer for transportation or transport certain cylinders (2P, 2Q, 39), portable tanks, cargo tanks and tank cars containing unodorized liquefied petroleum gases (LPG) unless the packagings are legibly marked NON-ODORIZED or NOT ODORIZED.

- Cylinders must be marked by the proper shipping name.

- Portable tanks must be marked on two opposing sides near the proper shipping name or the placards.

- Cargo tanks must be marked on two opposing sides near the proper shipping name or the placards.

- Tanks cars and multi-unit tank car tanks must be marked on two opposing sides near the proper shipping name or the placards. The marking may appear on a tank car or multi-unit tank car tank used for both unodorized and odorized LPG.

Additional marking requirements

Orientation arrows (172.312)

Non-bulk combination packages having inner packagings containing liquid hazardous materials, single packagings fitted with vents (mandatory January 1, 2008), or open cryogenic receptacles intended for the transport of refrigerated liquefied gases (mandatory January 1, 2008), must be legibly marked with package orientation markings that are similar to the illustration shown.

The arrows must be either black or red on white or other suitable contrasting background and commensurate with the size of the package (mandatory January 1, 2008). Depicting a rectangular border around the arrows is optional.

Arrow markings are not required on non-bulk packagings with:

- Inner packagings that are cylinders.
- Limited quantity or ORM-D flammable liquids in inner packagings of 1 L or less, except for transport by air.
- Limited quantity or ORM-D flammable liquids in inner packagings of 120 mL (4 fluid oz.) or less, when packed with sufficient absorption material to completely absorb the liquid contents, when transported by air.
- Liquids in manufactured articles (alcohol or mercury in thermometers) that are leak-tight in all orientations.
- Hermetically-sealed inner packagings.

Inhalation hazards and poisons (172.313)

Packagings containing materials poisonous-by-inhalation must be marked "INHALATION HAZARD," in addition to the required labels or placards or proper shipping name.

```
INHALATION
HAZARD
```

The marking is not required if the package already has a poison gas or inhalation hazard label or placard that displays the words "Inhalation Hazard."

The word "POISON" must be permanently marked on each non-bulk plastic outer packaging used as a single or composite packaging for Division 6.1 hazmat.

"PG III" may be marked adjacent to the POISON label on a package containing a Division 6.1 PG III hazmat.

Packages containing limited quantities (172.315)

Except for transportation by aircraft or as otherwise provided, a package containing a limited quantity of hazmat is not required to be marked with the proper shipping name, if it is marked with the identification number, preceded by the letters "UN" or "NA" and placed within a square-on-point border.

The ID number must:

- be durable, legible, and of a size relative to the package so it is readily visible; and

- be applied on at least one side or one end of the outer packaging.

The width of the line forming the square-on-point must be at least 2 mm, and the height of the ID number must be at least 6 mm.

When two or more hazardous materials with different ID numbers are in the same package, it must be marked with individual square-on-points, each with a single ID number, or a single square-on-point large enough to include each ID number.

ORM-Ds (172.316)

Non-bulk packagings containing a hazmat classed as "ORM-D" must be marked on at least one side or end with the ORM-D designation immediately following or below the proper shipping name.

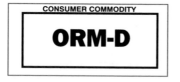

KEEP AWAY FROM HEAT handling mark (172.317)

For transportation by aircraft, each package containing Division 4.1 self-reactive substances or Division 5.2 organic peroxides must be marked with the KEEP AWAY FROM HEAT marking.

The marking must be durable, legible, and displayed on a background of contrasting color.

Marine pollutants (172.322)

Marine pollutants in bulk packagings of 3,785 L (1,000 gallons) or more must be marked on each side and each end with the marine pollutant marking. Bulk packagings less than 3,785 L (1,000 gallons) must be marked on two opposing sides.

However, a bulk packaging displaying a label or placard is not required to display the marking, except for transportation by vessel.

Non-bulk packaging containing marine pollutants transported by vessel must display the marine pollutant marking.

Infectious substances (172.323)

A bulk packaging containing a regulated medical waste must be marked with a BIOHAZARD marking:

- On two opposing sides or two ends other than the bottom if the packaging has a capacity of less than 3,785 L (1,000 gallons). The BIOHAZARD marking must measure at least 152.4 mm (6 inches) on each side and must be visible from the direction it faces.

- On each end and each side if the packaging has a capacity of 3,785 L (1,000 gallons) or more. The BIOHAZARD marking must measure at least 152.4 mm (6 inches) on each side and must be visible from the direction it faces.

For a bulk packaging contained in or on a transport vehicle or freight container, if the BIOHAZARD marking on the bulk packaging is not visible, the transport vehicle or freight container must be marked as required on each side and each end.

Marking

The background color for the BIOHAZARD marking must be orange and the symbol and letters must be black. Except for size, the BIOHAZARD marking must appear as follows:

The BIOHAZARD marking must be displayed on a background of contrasting color. It may be displayed on a plain white square-on-point configuration having the same outside dimensions as a placard.

Elevated temperature materials (172.325)

Except for bulk packagings containing molten aluminum or molten sulfur, a bulk packaging containing an elevated temperature material must be marked on two opposing sides with the word "HOT" in black or white Gothic lettering on a contrasting background. Packaging containing molten aluminum or molten sulfur must instead be marked "MOLTEN ALUMINUM" or "MOLTEN SULFUR," respectively.

You can also combine the "HOT" marking with the required ID number on a white square-on-point configuration. The ID number must be displayed in the center of the configuration and the word "HOT" may be displayed in the upper corner.

Overpacks (173.25)

Overpacks must be marked with the proper shipping name, ID number, and labeled for each hazmat contained inside, unless the marking and labels on the inside packagings are visible.

Overpacks must be marked with the word "OVERPACK" when specification packagings are required, unless the specification markings on the inside packagings are visible. Alternatively, until October 1, 2007, the overpack may be marked with a statement indicating that the "inside packages comply with prescribed specifications."

Orientation arrows must be marked on two opposing vertical sides of an overpack with the arrows pointing in the correct direction, and each package in the overpack must be packed with its filling hole(s) up.

Notes

Labeling
(Part 172, Subpart E)

Hazard warning labels are meant to communicate immediate warning of a hazmat's hazards. The colors and symbols on the various labels are designed to provide easy recognition of the hazard(s) a hazmat presents in transportation. Labeling requirements are targeted almost exclusively at non-bulk packaging. The responsibility for the label-

ing process belongs to the person offering the hazmat for transportation. However, the carrier also is responsible. The carrier must make sure that packages containing hazmat have been properly labeled according to the requirements before accepting and transporting them.

Label specifications (172.407)

Labels must be durable, weather resistant, and able to withstand, without deterioration or substantial change in color, a 30-day exposure to transport conditions.

Each diamond-shaped label must be at least 100 mm (3.9 inches) on each side, with each side also having a solid line inner border 5.0 to 6.3 mm (0.2 to 0.25 inch) from the edge of the label.

The hazard class/division number must be at least 6.3 mm (0.25 inch) and not greater than 12.7 mm (0.5 inch). If text indicating a hazard is displayed, the text must be shown in letters measuring at least 7.6 mm (0.3 inch) in height. The words "Spontaneously" and "When Wet" must be at least 5.1 mm (0.2 inch) in height, respectively, for SPONTANEOUSLY COMBUSTIBLE or DANGEROUS WHEN WET labels.

Labeling

The background color for the various labels must be as prescribed in 172.411 through 172.448, and the printing, inner border and symbol on each label must be as shown.

In most cases, the symbol, test, numbers, and border must be black. However, white may be used on a label with a one color background of green, red, or blue. White must be used for the text and class number for the CORROSIVE label.

Primary and subsidiary labels (172.402)

There are two types of hazard warning labels. A primary hazard label indicates a hazmat's most hazardous property; a subsidiary hazard label indicates other less hazardous properties.

Subsidiary labels have numbers in the lower corner, just like primary labels.

You may see subsidiary labels that have no number in the lower corner. Subsidiary labels without a number in the lower corner can not be used in domestic transportation starting October 1, 2005.

When primary and subsidiary hazard labels are required together, they must be displayed next to each other (within 6 inches).

Determining labels (172.101 & 172.400)

The Hazardous Materials Table is used for determining appropriate hazard warning labels.

First, locate the proper shipping name in Column 2 of the Table.

Then, refer to Column 6 for the appropriate label code(s).

The first label code indicates the hazmat's primary hazard. Any additional label codes listed are subsidiary hazards. Usually the label code is the same as the hazard class or division for the label. You can also use the Label Substitution Table in 172.101(g). There is another table located in 172.400, that should be used in determining additional subsidiary labels.

For the 6.1 label code, there are two possible labels. Hazmat that has a Hazard Zone A or B requires a POISON INHALATION HAZARD label; any other 6.1 hazmat will require a POISON label.

Exceptions (172.400a)

As mentioned earlier, not all non-bulk packages of hazmat need to be labeled. Labels are not required on:

- A cylinder or Dewar flask (173.320) containing a Division 2.1, 2.2, or 2.3 material; that is not overpacked; and that is durably and legibly marked in accordance with CGA Pamphlet C-7, Appendix A.

- A package or unit of military explosives, including ammunition, shipped by or on behalf of the U.S. Department of Defense (DOD) when in freight container-load, car-load, or truck-load shipments, if loaded and unloaded by the shipper or DOD, or in unitized or palletized break-bulk shipments by cargo vessel under charter to DOD, if at least one required label is displayed on each unitized or palletized load.

- A package of hazmat, other than ammunition, that is loaded and unloaded under the supervision of DOD personnel and is escorted by DOD personnel in a separate vehicle.

- A compressed gas cylinder that is permanently mounted in or on a transport vehicle.

- A freight container, aircraft unit load device, or portable tank that is placarded in accordance with or identified as provided in the International Civil Aviation Organization (ICAO) Technical Instructions.

- An overpack or unit load device in or on which labels that represent the hazard(s) inside are visible.

- A package of low specific-activity radioactive material when being transported in a conveyance assigned for the exclusive use of the consignor under 173.427(a)(6).

- A package containing a material classed as ORM-D, provided the package does not contain any other material classed as a hazmat that requires labeling.

- A package containing a combustible liquid.

Label placement (172.406)

A label must be printed or affixed to the outside surface of a package containing hazmat, but not on the bottom. Labels should not be hidden or concealed; they must be easily seen. Labels must be on a background of contrasting color or have a dotted or solid line outer border. You must also put the label on the same side and near the proper shipping name, when possible.

Duplicate labeling is not usually required on a package, only one of each required label is necessary. However, duplicate labeling may be required for larger packages and radioactive packages. See 172.406(e).

What if the package is very small? A label may be printed on or put on a securely affixed tag or affixed by other suitable means to:

- a package that is smaller than the required label if it is not a radioactive hazmat;

- a cylinder; and

- a package that has an irregular surface.

Mixed and consolidated packaging (172.404)

Hazmat with different hazard classes packed in the same packaging, or within the same outside container or overpack, must be labeled for each of the different hazard classes.

Also, an outside container or overpack must be labeled as required for each class of hazmat when two or more packages with compatible hazardous materials are put in the outside container or overpack.

Label modifications (172.405)

Text indicating a hazard is not required on Class 1, 2, 3, 4, 5, 6, and 8 primary or subsidiary labels.

The OXIDIZER label may be modified to display the word "OXYGEN" and the class number "2," which can then be used instead of the NON-FLAMMABLE GAS and OXIDIZER labels for packages with the proper shipping names "Oxygen, compressed" or "Oxygen, refrigerated liquid." The word "OXYGEN" must appear on the label.

The POISON label may be modified to display the text "PG III" below the midline of the label for packages containing a Division 6.1, Packing Group III hazmat.

ORGANIC PEROXIDE label (172.427)

HM-215I revised the ORGANIC PEROXIDE label. The new label reflects the fact that organic peroxides are highly flammable and enables transport workers to readily distinguish peroxides from oxidizers. Labels meeting the specifications in effect on December 31, 2006, are authorized to continue to be displayed until January 1, 2011.

Except for size and color, the ORGANIC PEROXIDE label must be as follows:

The background on the label must be red in the top half and yellow in the lower half. White may also be used for the symbol for the ORGANIC PEROXIDE label.

Use of the new label will become mandatory on January 1, 2011.

Placarding
(Part 172, Subpart F)

Placards are often confused with labels, simply because they look so much alike. Placards are much larger and are usually placed on much larger packages.

The purpose of placards is very similar to the purpose of labels. Placards communicate the hazards associated with various materials in transportation, and also provide emergency personnel with the information they need when incidents occur — two good reasons why it is important to make sure you select and display the right placards.

Placarding requirements (172.504)

Each bulk packaging, freight container, unit load device, transport vehicle, or rail car containing hazmat must be placarded, with some exceptions.

To determine the placards required, you must know:

- Whether the packaging is bulk or non-bulk.

- The hazard category (class, division, packing group, or description), and subsidiary hazard(s), if any.

- The weight of non-bulk packages in each hazard category.

Table 1 (172.504)

The most dangerous hazmat categories are located in Table 1. Any quantity of hazmat in the categories listed in Table 1 must be placarded.

Table 1		
Category of material (Hazard class or division number and additional description, as appropriate)	Placard name	Placard design section reference (§)
1.1	EXPLOSIVES 1.1	172.522
1.2	EXPLOSIVES 1.2	172.522
1.3	EXPLOSIVES 1.3	172.522
2.3	POISON GAS	172.540
4.3	DANGEROUS WHEN WET	172.548
5.2 (Organic peroxide, Type B, liquid or solid, temperature controlled).	ORGANIC PEROXIDE	172.552
6.1 (Material poisonous by inhalation (see §171.8 of this subchapter))	POISON INHALATION HAZARD	172.555
7 (Radioactive Yellow III label only)	RADIOACTIVE[1]	172.556

[1]RADIOACTIVE placard also required for exclusive use shipments of low specific activity material and surface contaminated objects transported in accordance with 173.427(b)(4) and (5) or (c) of this subchapter.

Table 2 (172.504)

The remaining hazard categories are in Table 2. Any quantity of hazmat in Table 2 must also be placarded, with some exceptions allowed in the regulations.

Table 2		
Category of material (Hazard class or division number and additional description, as appropriate)	Placard name	Placard design section reference (§)
1.4	EXPLOSIVES 1.4	172.523
1.5	EXPLOSIVES 1.5	172.524
1.6	EXPLOSIVES 1.6	172.525
2.1	FLAMMABLE GAS	172.532
2.2	NON-FLAMMABLE GAS	172.528
3	FLAMMABLE	172.542
Combustible liquid	COMBUSTIBLE	172.544
4.1	FLAMMABLE SOLID	172.546
4.2	SPONTANEOUSLY COMBUSTIBLE	172.547
5.1	OXIDIZER	172.550
5.2 (Other than organic peroxide, Type B, liquid or solid, temperature controlled)	ORGANIC PEROXIDE	172.552
6.1 (Other than material poisonous by inhalation)	POISON	172.554
6.2	(None)	
8	CORROSIVE	172.558
9	CLASS 9 (see §172.504(f)(9))	172.560
ORM-D	(None)	

Placarding exceptions (172.504)

1,001 lb rule (172.504)

A transport vehicle or freight container that has less than 454 kg (1,001 lb) aggregate gross weight of hazmat in non-bulk packages, covered by Table 2, is not required to display placards. This exception does not apply to bulk packages or materials with subsidiary hazards that must be placarded.

DANGEROUS placard (172.504)

A transport vehicle, rail car, freight container, or unit load device containing non-bulk packagings of two or more categories of Table 2 hazmat may display a DANGEROUS placard instead of the separate placards specified in Table 2.

When 1,000 kg (2,205 lb) or more of one hazard category is loaded at one facility, on one vehicle, rail car, freight container, or unit load device, the DANGEROUS placard can not be used instead of the placard specified in Table 2.

For example, when three or more different categories of Table 2 hazmat are in one vehicle, rail car, freight container, or unit load device, and one material is over 1,000 kg (2,205 lb) and an individual class placard from Table 2 is required, the DANGEROUS placard may still be displayed for other Table 2 categories falling under the 1,000 kg (2,205 lb) limit.

Residue (172.504)

A non-bulk packaging containing just the residue of a Table 2 hazmat does not have to be included when determining placards for a transport vehicle, rail car, freight container, or unit load device.

Freight containers/unit load devices (172.512)

A motor vehicle transporting freight containers or aircraft unit load devices that are not required to be placarded is not required to display placards.

Freight containers and unit load devices being transported for delivery to a consignee immediately after an air or water shipment are also allowed to use the exception for less than 454 kg (1,001 lb) of Table 2 materials.

A freight container or aircraft unit load device that is only transported by air and is prepared according to Part 7, Chapter 2, Section 2.7 of the ICAO Technical Instructions is not required to be placarded.

Class 1 (explosives) (172.504)

When more than one division placard is required for Class 1 materials on a transport vehicle, rail car, freight container, or unit load device, only the placard representing the lowest division number must be displayed.

> **Example:** *A transport vehicle carrying Division 1.3, 1.4, and 1.5 materials could be placarded for Division 1.3.*

For shipments of Class 1 materials by aircraft or vessel, the applicable compatibility group letter must be displayed on the required placards.

The EXPLOSIVES 1.4 placard is not required for Division 1.4 Compatibility Group S (1.4S) materials not required to be labeled 1.4S.

Flammable/combustible (172.504)

A FLAMMABLE placard may be used instead of a COMBUSTIBLE placard on a cargo tank or portable tank, or a compartment tank containing flammable and combustible liquids.

Gases (172.504)

A NON-FLAMMABLE GAS placard is not required on a motor vehicle containing a non-flammable gas if the vehicle also contains flammable gas or oxygen and is placarded FLAMMABLE GAS or OXYGEN, as required.

The OXYGEN placard may be used for domestic shipments of "Oxygen, compressed," or "Oxygen, refrigerated liquid," in place of a NON-FLAMMABLE GAS placard.

Oxidizers (172.504)

OXIDIZER placards are not required for Division 5.1 materials on freight containers, unit load devices, transport vehicles, or rail cars that also contain Division 1.1 or 1.2 materials and that are placarded with EXPLOSIVES 1.1 or 1.2 placards, as required.

For transportation by transport vehicle or rail car only, an OXIDIZER placard is not required for Division 5.1 materials on a transport vehicle, rail car, or freight container that also contains Division 1.5 materials and is placarded with EXPLOSIVES 1.5 placards, as required.

Class 9 (172.504)

CLASS 9 placards are not required for domestic transportation, including that portion of international transportation that occurs within the U.S.

Poisons (172.504)

For domestic transportation, a POISON placard is not required on a transport vehicle or freight container required to display a POISON INHALATION HAZARD or POISON GAS placard.

Prohibited & permissive placarding (172.502)

"Drive Safely" is a perfect example of prohibited placarding. Any sign, slogan, or advertisement with color, design, shape, or content that could be confused with any DOT placard is not allowed.

You may not display any DOT placard on a packaging, freight container, unit load device, motor vehicle, or rail car unless the:

- Material offered or transported is a hazmat.

- Placard displayed represents a hazard of the material being offered or transported.

- Placarding is in compliance with the regulations.

Placarding may be displayed for hazmat, even when not required, if done according to the requirements.

Placard placement (172.516)

Placards on a motor vehicle or rail car must be clearly visible from the direction it faces, except from the direction of another transport vehicle or rail car to which the motor vehicle or rail car is coupled.

Required placarding for the front of a motor vehicle may be on the front of a truck-tractor instead of, or in addition to, the placarding on the front of the cargo body attached to the truck-tractor.

Each placard on a transport vehicle, bulk packaging, freight container, or aircraft unit load device must:

- Be securely attached or put in a placard holder.

- Be on a background of contrasting color, or have a dotted or solid line outer border that contrasts with the background color.

- Be clear of appurtenances and devices like ladders, pipes, doors, and tarps.

- Be located so dirt or water is not directed to it from the wheels of the transport vehicle.

- Be located away from any marking (at least 3 inches) that could reduce its effectiveness.

- Have the words or ID number printed on it displayed horizontally, reading from left to right.

- Be maintained in a condition to insure its effectiveness will not be reduced.

ORGANIC PEROXIDE placard (172.552)

HM-215I revised the ORGANIC PEROXIDE placard. The new placard reflects the fact that organic peroxides are highly flammable and enables transport workers to readily distinguish peroxides from oxidizers. Placards meeting the specifications in effect on December 31, 2006, are authorized to continue to be displayed until January 1, 2014, for transportation by highway and until January 1, 2011, for transportation by rail, vessel or aircraft.

Except for size and color, the ORGANIC PEROXIDE placard must be as follows:

The background on the placard must be red in the top half and yellow in the lower half. The text, division number, and inner border must be black; the symbol may be either black or white.

Use of the new placard will become mandatory January 1, 2011, for transportation by rail, vessel or aircraft; January 1, 2014, for transportation by highway.

Notes

Incident Reporting
(171.15 & 171.16)

Even when all possible precautions are taken, accidents
and incidents can and will
happen. When hazmat is
involved, the risks to health
and the environment are even
greater. The Hazardous
Materials Regulations require
"hazmat employers" to train
their "hazmat employees" on
the proper procedures for

responding quickly and safely to leaks, spills, and other such emer-
gencies. The regulations also require carriers of all modes to provide proper notification of hazardous materials incidents. This
section will look at PHMSA's requirements for incident reporting,
and will address some of the modal-specific requirements for accidents involving hazardous materials.

Carrier incident contact (172.606)

Each carrier who transports or accepts for transportation a hazardous material that requires a shipping paper must instruct the
operator of the vehicle, train, aircraft, or vessel to contact them
(the carrier) in the event of an incident involving hazmat. Each
operator of a vehicle, train, aircraft, or vessel must contact their
employer (carrier) when there is an incident involving hazmat.

The carrier is responsible for reporting any incident that occurs during loading, unloading, transportation, or temporary storage. An "incident" is any situation requiring a telephone report as specified in Section 171.15, or any unintentional release of hazmat from a package (including a tank). The type of report that must be filed — telephone and/or written — will be dictated by the incident's severity.

Accidents vs. incidents

It is important to understand that an "incident" may, or may not have been, the result of an accident. Each mode of transportation has specific accident reporting procedures that may apply to incidents.

Telephone report (171.15)

As soon as possible, the person in possession of the hazmat must notify authorities of each incident that occurs during the course of transportation (including loading, unloading, and temporary storage) when, as a direct result of hazmat:

- A person is killed.

- A person receives injuries requiring admittance to a hospital.

- Evacuation of the general public occurs, lasting one hour or more.

- One or more major transportation arteries or facilities are closed or shut down for one hour or more.

- The operational flight pattern or routine of an aircraft is altered.

- Fire, breakage, spillage, or suspected radioactive contamination occurs involving a shipment of radioactive material.

- Fire, breakage, spillage, or suspected contamination occurs involving an infectious substance other than a diagnostic specimen or regulated medical waste.

- A release of a marine pollutant in a quantity exceeding 450 L (119 gallons) for liquids, or 400 kg (882 pounds) for solids.

- A situation exists of such a nature (like a continued threat to life) that, in the judgment of the person in possession of the hazmat, it should be reported even though it does not meet one of the other conditions.

The agency that the carrier is to notify will vary depending on the mode of transportation and the type of material involved. The applicable telephone numbers are listed below.

Mode or Material	Who to Notify
Rail, water & highway	National Response Center at **1-800-424-8802**
Air	Nearest FAA Regional or Field Security Office by telephone
Infectious substances	Director of the Centers for Disease Control (CDC) at **1-800-232-0124**

When calling to report a hazardous material incident, be prepared to provide the following:

- ✓ Name of reporter.

- ✓ Name and address of person represented by reporter.

- ✓ Telephone number where reporter can be reached.

- ✓ Date, time, and location of the hazmat incident.

- ✓ Extent of injuries, if any.

- ✓ Classification, proper shipping name, and quantity of hazmat involved.

- Type of incident and nature of hazmat involvement and whether a continuing danger to life exists.

In addition to the telephone notification requirements, anyone in charge of facilities (including transport vehicles, vessels, and aircraft) is required to report any release of a hazardous substance in a quantity that equals or exceeds its reportable quantity (RQ). The report must be made to the U.S. Coast Guard National Response Center at (800) 424-8802 or (202) 267-2675, as soon as there is knowledge of the release.

Written report (171.16)

Within 30 days of the date of discovery, the person in physical possession of the hazmat must file a written "Hazardous Materials Incident Report" for each incident that:

- Involves any of the circumstances listed for a telephone report.

- Involves an unintentional release of a hazardous material or the discharge of any quantity of hazardous waste.

- Involves a specification cargo tank with a capacity of 1,000 gallons or greater containing any hazmat suffers structural damage to the lading retention system or damage that requires repair to a system intended to protect the lading retention system, even if there is no release of hazardous material.

- Involves an undeclared hazmat.

Unless a telephone report is required, a written report is not required for:

- a release of a minimal amount of material from—

    - a vent, for materials for which venting is authorized;

    - the routine operation of a seal, pump, compressor, or valve; or

    - connection or disconnection of loading or unloading lines, provided the release does not result in property damage.

- an unintentional release of hazardous material when—

    ○ the material is properly classed as—

        - ORM-D; or

        - a Packing Group III material in Class or Division 3, 4, 5, 6.1, 8, or 9;

    ○ each package has a capacity of less than 20 liters (5.2 gallons) for liquids or less than 30 kg (66 pounds) for solids;

    ○ the total aggregate release is less than 20 liters (5.2 gallons) for liquids or less than 30 kg (66 pounds) for solids; and

    ○ the material is not—

        - offered for transportation or transported by aircraft;

        - a hazardous waste; or

        - an undeclared hazardous material.

Incident Reporting

The "Hazardous Materials Incident Report" must be completed using DOT Form 5800.1 (01/2004), and sent to:

Information Systems Manager, PHH-63
Pipeline and Hazardous Materials Safety Administration
Department of Transportation
Washington, DC 20590-0001

Alternatively, an electronic report can be completed on the internet at http: hazmat.dot.gov.

A copy of the "Hazardous Materials Incident Report" must be retained for a period of two (2) years at the reporting person's principal place of business.

If the written or electronic report is maintained at a different location, it must be made available at the reporting person's principal place of business within 24 hours of a request for the report by the Department of Transportation.

A Hazardous Materials Incident Report must be updated within one year of the date of occurrence if:

- a death results from injuries caused by a hazmat;

- there was a misidentification of the hazmat or package information on a prior incident report;

- damage, loss or related cost that was not known when the initial report was filed becomes known; or

- damage, loss or related cost changes by $25,000 or more, or 10 percent of the prior total estimate, whichever is greater.

Notes

ping papers, away from packages containing hazmat, and in a location immediately accessible in the event of an incident.

Acceptable methods

The most common methods for providing the required emergency response information include:

- Listing it directly on the shipping papers.

- Keeping a copy of the Emergency Response Guidebook with the shipping papers.

- Keeping a copy of the appropriate guide page from the Emergency Response Guidebook with the shipping papers.

- In a document that includes both the material's basic description and technical name(s), if any.

- Keeping a copy of the material's MSDS (Material Safety Data Sheet) with the shipping papers. The material's basic description and technical name(s), if any, must be included.

Emergency Response Guidebook (ERG)

The ERG was developed by Canadian, Mexican, and United States agencies to assist first responders at the scene of a transportation incident involving hazardous materials. It enables them to quickly identify the specific or general classification of the material involved, and protect themselves and the general public during the initial response phase.

Although the ERG was developed for first responders it may be used to satisfy PHMSA's emergency response information requirements.

The ERG consists of four colored sections:

- The **yellow** section lists hazmat in numerical order. It can be used to find the appropriate "guide number" if the material's assigned identification number is known.

- The **blue** section lists hazmat in alphabetical order. It can be used to find the appropriate "guide number" if the material's proper shipping name is known.

- The **orange** section consists of numbered "guides" that list a material's potential hazards and emergency action procedures.

- The **green** section lists suggested distances for protecting people from spill areas involving hazmat that produces poisonous effects when inhaled. This section must be referenced if the hazmat entry is highlighted in either the yellow or blue section.

Keeping an ERG with the shipping papers is a good way to satisfy the emergency response information requirements. If you are going to use a copy of the appropriate guide page to meet the emergency responder information requirements be sure to add the material's basic description and technical name(s), if any, to the copy.

Notes

Training and Security
(Part 172, Subparts H & I)

Training is one of the more important things a hazmat company can do to insure the security of hazardous materials.  Now that the topic of security is directly addressed in the regulations, compliance with the requirements will help to improve security needed in the hazmat transportation process. When a hazmat employee is thoroughly trained, anything out of the ordinary should immediately raise a red flag.

The Hazardous Materials Regulations require training covering specific subject areas for all hazmat employees. The requirements are detailed in Subpart H of Part 172. Additional training requirements specifically for drivers who transport hazardous materials by highway are detailed in Section 177.816.

Security awareness training (Part 172, Subpart H)

The Research and Special Programs Administration (RSPA), the predecessor agency to PHMSA, established requirements (HM-232) to enhance the security of hazardous materials transported in commerce. Shippers and carriers of hazardous materials must make sure all hazmat employees receive training that includes a security component.

Security awareness training requirements are found in 49 CFR 172 Subpart H. Current employees must have security awareness training at their next recurrent training or no later than March 24, 2006. New hires need to be trained within 90 days of employment.

Each hazmat employee must receive training that will provide:

- An awareness of security risks associated with hazmat transportation.

- Methods designed to enhance transportation security.

- A component covering how to recognize and respond to possible security threats.

Security plans and in-depth security training (Part 172, Subpart H & I)

If your company registers with the federal government to ship or carry hazardous materials, a security plan may need to be completed. The security plan must include an assessment of possible transportation security risks and appropriate measures to address the assessed risks.

The training must include:

- Company security objectives.

- Specific security procedures.

- Employee responsibilities.

- Actions to take in the event of a security breach.

- The organizational security structure.

Security risks and security awareness

Security is important throughout the entire hazmat transportation process. If you are involved in any part of the process, it is up to you to make sure your job is done safely and securely.

Security will vary from one location to another, depending on how dangerous the hazmat is, and what kind of hazards it might pose if it fell into the wrong hands. Non-bulk packages of charcoal lighter fluid shipping out of one facility would present less of a security risk than cargo tanks filled with gasoline or a deadly poison.

Try to identify potential areas of vulnerability and security risks associated with your job environment. Some will be easily recognized. Others could be harder to spot. Your supervisor may conduct a vulnerability assessment prior to your security awareness training. Be ready to provide input about potential risks and areas of vulnerability you have identified.

Security checks at your business might include:

- Making sure all hazmat storage areas are secure.
- Requiring ID cards/badges for access to hazmat areas.
- Keeping track of hazmat removed from secure locations.
- Using locks, alarms and/or surveillance cameras as protective measures in hazmat areas.
- Making sure there is adequate lighting.
- Protecting high-risk hazmat areas with guards.
- Conducting security checks of personnel and vehicles.
- Conducting security checks of hazmat packages and shipping documents.

As a driver, security becomes an even larger issue. Out on the road, you have to be constantly aware of your surroundings, and keep an eye out for anything that might appear out of the ordinary.

Before you leave the loading area, make sure you:

- ✓ Have proper identification.
- ✓ Have all necessary licenses, endorsements, and permits.
- ✓ Have shipping papers and emergency response information in order and easy to access.
- ✓ Know the route you will be driving.

Training and Security

✓ Know what to do in case of an emergency and who to contact.

Once on the road:

✓ Be prepared to be stopped by enforcement officials and ask for identification.

✓ Avoid high population and congestion areas.

✓ Avoid tunnels and bridges.

✓ Don't use the same route every time.

✓ Use designated hazmat routes.

✓ Deliver your load without delay.

✓ Keep your vehicle locked and secure and attended at all times.

✓ Talk regularly with your dispatcher, but don't discuss your load on the CB.

Potential threats and potential targets may exist, not only on the job, but in your community, and out on the road, too. The need for a heightened sense of awareness is always present. Don't let your guard down. If you do, you and others could be at risk.

Stay alert and aware. Report any suspicious activities to your supervisor or the proper authorities as soon as possible.

Notes

Notes

Loading/Unloading
(Part 177, Subpart B)

The hazmat regulations contain specific requirements for the proper loading, unloading, transport, and storage of hazardous materials. The rules are modal-specific and are designed to protect anyone involved with the shipment, as well as those who may come into contact with it. The requirements include provisions for quantity limitations, segregation, monitoring, load securement, vehicle positioning, and routing. To ensure complete compliance, you must always reference the applicable parts of the regulations. Loading and unloading may be an every day part of your job, but it is important to make sure it is done correctly.

Carriage by highway (Parts 172, 177 & 397)

Unless specifically excepted, each carrier (private, common, or contract), including any connecting carrier, must comply with the applicable loading and unloading requirements contained in Part 177. The requirements also apply to anyone involved with the loading and/or unloading process.

Each carrier has to comply with the driving and parking rules contained in Part 397. The rules include provisions for attendance and surveillance, parking, smoking, fueling, tire inspections, and routing.

Each carrier also has to comply with the carrier information contact requirements in Section 172.606. This section requires that certain information be provided on a dropped or disconnected trailer/container.

Shipping paper accessibility (177.817)

Shipping papers must be readily available to, and recognizable by, authorities in the event of an accident or inspection.

The driver and carrier must:

- Clearly distinguish the hazmat shipping paper from other papers by tabbing it, or having it appear first.

- Keep the shipping paper within immediate reach while restrained by the lap belt and at the vehicle's controls, and visible to someone entering the driver's compartment or in a holder mounted to the inside of the driver's side door.

- Keep the shipping paper in a driver's side door pouch or on the driver's seat when not at the vehicle controls.

General requirements (177.834)

In Subpart B of Part 177, the regulations state the general and class-specific requirements for the loading and unloading of hazmat shipments. The majority of the general requirements are summarized as follows:

- Packages must be secured against shifting, including relative motion between packages, within the vehicle under conditions normally encountered during transport. Packages having valves or other fittings must be loaded in a manner to minimize the likelihood of damage during transportation.

- Smoking on or near a vehicle — or carrying any flame, lighted cigar, pipe, or cigarette — is prohibited during the loading and unloading of Class 1 (explosive), Division 2.1 (flammable gas) materials, Class 3 (flammable liquid), Class 4 (flammable solid), and Class 5 (oxidizing).

- The vehicle's hand brake must be securely set and all other reasonable precautions taken to prevent the vehicle from moving during loading and unloading.

- Any tools that are likely to damage or adversely affect a package, container, or closure must not be used.

- Containers in transit should be protected from an undue rise in temperature.

- Containers and their contents must be protected from tampering between point of origin and point of billed destination. Discharge of contents must not be made prior to removal from the motor vehicle.

- The loading and unloading of a cargo tank must be attended at all times by a qualified person. ("Qualified person" and "attend" are both defined in Section 177.834(i).)

- The use of cargo heaters during the transport of flammable and explosive hazardous materials must be in compliance with Section 177.834(l).

Class-specific requirements

Whenever a highway shipment of hazardous materials is loaded or unloaded, it must be done according to the general requirements detailed in Section 177.834, as well as with the specific requirements for that class.

The requirements can be found in Subpart B, as follows:

Class 1 (explosive) — 177.835

Class 2 (gases) — 177.840

Class 3 (flammable liquid) — 177.837

Class 4 (flammable solid), Division 4.2 (pyrophoric liquid), and Class 5 (oxidizer) — 177.838

Division 6.1 (poisonous) and Division 2.3 (poisonous gas) — 177.841

Class 7 (radioactive) materials — 177.842

Class 8 (corrosive) materials — 177.839

Driving and parking rules (Part 397, Subpart A)

The driving and parking rules contained in Part 397 apply to every motor carrier transporting hazmat in a motor vehicle that is required to be marked or placarded.

In general, the rules are:

- Motor vehicles must be driven and parked in compliance with the laws, ordinances, and regulations of the jurisdiction in which they are being operated.

- Except as provided in Section 397.5, a motor vehicle containing Division 1.1, 1.2, or 1.3 (explosive) materials must be attended at all times by its driver or a qualified representative of the carrier.

- A motor vehicle that contains hazmat other than Division 1.1, 1.2, or 1.3 materials and is located on a public street or highway, or the shoulder of a public highway, must be attended by its driver. However, the vehicle is not required to be attended while its driver is performing duties which are incident and necessary to his/her duties as the vehicle's operator.

- A motor vehicle which contains Division 1.1, 1.2, or 1.3 materials must not be parked:

    - On or within 5 feet of the traveled portion of a public street or highway.

    - On private property, without knowledge and consent of the person in charge of the property.

    - Within 300 feet of a bridge, tunnel, dwelling, building, or other place where people work or congregate, except for brief periods when the necessities of operation require the vehicle to be parked and make it impractical to park in any other place.

- A motor vehicle which contains hazardous materials other than Division 1.1, 1.2, or 1.3 must not be parked on or within 5 feet of the traveled portion of a public street or highway, except for brief periods when the necessities of operation require the vehicle to be parked and make it impractical to park in any other place.

- A motor vehicle must not be operated near an open fire, unless the driver has taken precautions to make sure the vehicle can safely pass without stopping.

- No person may smoke or carry a lighted cigarette, cigar, or pipe within 25 feet of a vehicle that contains flammable, oxidizing, or explosive materials, or their residues.

- When fueling, the engine must be shut off, and the person in control of fueling must be at the point where the fuel tank is filled.

- The tires of a motor vehicle must be examined at the beginning of each trip and each time the vehicle is parked.

Carrier information contact (172.606)

When a transport vehicle contains hazmat that requires a shipping paper, and the vehicle is separated from its motive power and parked at a location other than a facility operated by the consignor or consignee or a facility subject to the emergency response information requirements in 172.602(c)(2), the carrier shall:

- Mark the vehicle with the telephone number of the motor carrier on the outside front near the brake hose and electrical connections, or on a label, tag, or sign attached at the brake hose or electrical connection; or

Loading/Unloading

- Have the shipping paper and emergency response information readily available on the transport vehicle; or

- Mark the transport vehicle with an orange panel, a placard, or a plain white square-on-point configuration with the identification numbers of each loaded hazmat. The placard or marking must be visible on the outside of the vehicle.

Notes

Notes

Load Segregation
(177.848)

The segregation of hazmat is another important step to make sure nothing happens to endanger life or property during the transportation process. It is your responsibility to be familiar with the segregation requirements.

For highway transportation, the segregation requirements apply to hazmat that fall into one or more hazard classes, and are:

- In packages that require labels,

- In a compartment within a multi-compartmented cargo tank (subject to the restrictions of Section 173.33), or

- In a portable tank loaded in a transport vehicle or freight container.

Hazmat must be loaded, transported, and stored only as specified in the regulations. In addition to the following tables, specific provisions prohibit cyanides, cyanide mixtures or solutions from being stored, loaded, and transported with acids if a mixture of the materials would generate hydrogen cyanide, and Division 4.2 materials may not be stored, loaded, and transported with Class 8 liquids.

Load Segregation

Segregation Table For Hazardous Materials																			
Class or division	Notes	1.1 1.2	1.3	1.4	1.5	1.6	2.1	2.2	2.3 gas Zone A	2.3 gas Zone B	3	4.1	4.2	4.3	5.1	5.2	6.1 liquids PG 1 Zone A	7	8 liquids only
Explosives ..... 1.1 and 1.2	A	*	*	*	*	*	X	X	X	X	X	X	X	X	X	X	X	X	X
Explosives 1.3		*	*	*	*	*	X		X	X	X		X	X	X	X	X		X
Explosives 1.4		*	*	*	*	*	O		O	O	O		O				O		O
Very insensitive 1.5	A	*	*	*	*	*	X	X	X	X	X	X	X	X	X	X	X	X	X
Extremely insensitive 1.6 explosives.		*	*	*	*	*													
Flammable gases 2.1		X	X	O	X				X	O							O	O	
Non-toxic, non-flammable gases. 2.2		X			X														
Poisonous gas Zone A 2.3		X	X	O	X		X				X	X	X	X	X	X			X
Poisonous gas Zone B 2.3		X	X	O	X		O				O	O	O	O	O	O			O
Flammable liquids 3		X	X	O	X			X	O						O		X		
Flammable solids 4.1		X			X			X	O						X		X		O
Spontaneously combustible materials. 4.2		X	X	O	X			X	O						X		X		X
Dangerous when wet materials. 4.3		X	X		X			X	O						X		X		O
Oxidizers 5.1	A	X	X		X			X	O	O							X		O
Organic peroxides 5.2		X	X		X			X	O						X		X		O
Poisonous liquids PG I 6.1 Zone A.		X	X	O	X		O				X	X	X	X	X	X			X
Radioactive materials .. 7		X			X		O												
Corrosive liquids 8		X	X	O	X			X	O			O	X	O	O	O	X		

To use the Segregation Table:

- Locate the hazard classes or divisions of the materials in question — one in the vertical column, the other in the horizontal row.

- Follow each to the location where they intersect.

- The codes at the intersection are defined as follows:

Code	Meaning
Blank	There are no restrictions. The materials may be loaded or stored together.
X	The materials may not be loaded, transported, or stored together.
O	The materials may not be loaded, transported, or stored together unless separated in a manner that — in the event of leakage — there would be no commingling of the materials under circumstances normal to transportation.
*	The segregation of Class 1 (explosive) materials is governed by the Compatibility Table for Class 1 (explosive) materials in Section 177.848(f).
A	Not withstanding the "X", ammonium nitrate (UN1942) and ammonium nitrate fertilizer may be loaded or stored with Division 1.1 or 1.5 materials.

Additionally, Class 1 (explosive) materials may only be loaded, stored, and transported together as provided in the Compatibility Table.

Compatibility Group	A	B	C	D	E	F	G	H	J	K	L	N	S
A.................		X	X	X	X	X	X	X	X	X	X	X	X
B.................	X		X	4	X	X	X	X	X	X	X	X	$4/5$
C.................	X	X		2	2	X	X	X	X	X	X	3	$4/5$
D.................	X	4	2		2	X	X	X	X	X	X	3	$4/5$
E.................	X	X	2	2		X	X	X	X	X	X	3	$4/5$
F.................	X	X	X	X	X		X	X	X	X	X	X	$4/5$
G.................	X	X	X	X	X	X		X	X	X	X	X	$4/5$
H.................	X	X	X	X	X	X	X		X	X	X	X	$4/5$
J.................	X	X	X	X	X	X	X	X		X	X	X	$4/5$
K.................	X	X	X	X	X	X	X	X	X		X	X	$4/5$
L.................	X	X	X	X	X	X	X	X	X	X	1	X	X
N.................	X	X	3	3	3	X	X	X	X	X	X		$4/5$
S.................	X	$4/5$	$4/5$	$4/5$	$4/5$	$4/5$	$4/5$	$4/5$	$4/5$	$4/5$	X	$4/5$	

Compatibility Table For Class 1 (Explosive) Materials

In this table, the codes are defined as follows:

Code	Meaning
Blank	No restrictions apply.
X	Explosives of different compatibility groups may not be carried on the same transport vehicle.
1	An explosive from compatibility group L shall only be carried on the same transport vehicle with an identical explosive.
2	Any combination of explosives from compatibility groups C, D, or E is assigned to compatibility group E.
3	Any combination of explosives from compatibility groups C, D, or E, with those in compatibility group N, is assigned to compatibility group D.
4	Refer to Section 177.835(g) when transporting detonators.
5	Division 1.4S fireworks may not be loaded on the same transport vehicle with Division 1.1 or 1.2 materials.

Notes

Packaging
(Part 178, Subpart L)

The way that a hazmat is packaged can have a signifi-cant impact on how safely the material can be transported in commerce.  The Research and Special Programs Administra-tion (RSPA), the predecessor agency to PHMSA, estab-lished very specific require-ments for all bulk and non-bulk packagings. The requirements are designed to make sure the packaging selected is appropriate for the hazmat and can stand up to the conditions normally encountered in transport. The non-bulk packaging requirements — based on the *UN Recom-mendations* — are complex and involve many different parts of the regulations.

Unless otherwise stated, or exceptions are authorized, the packaging requirements are the same for all modes of trans-port. Also, while most of the non-bulk requirements are based on the *UN Recommendations*, the regulations do contain some provisions that are only applicable to domestic transport. That means compliance with the provisions will not guarantee acceptance by regulatory bodies outside the United States.

The responsibility for packaging a hazmat rests with the individ-ual offering the material for transport. The responsibility includes:

- Selecting the right packaging for the material — taking into account its quantity and chemical composition, and the desired method of transport.

- Complying with special provisions and/or quantity limi-tations listed for the hazmat.

- Complying with general requirements for packaging, as well as the requirements for bulk or non-bulk pack-aging, as appropriate.

- Making sure the selected packaging meets performance test requirements and detailed specifications.

- Assembling and securing all components of the packaging correctly.

- Making sure the packaging is properly identified (i.e., marked, labeled, and placarded) before it is offered to the carrier for transport.

In addition to authorizing the use of specific packagings for hazmat, the regulations contain detailed specifications as to how the packagings must be constructed, as well as how they must perform during transport. To understand the various requirements, however, it is first necessary to understand several key terms.

Non-bulk and bulk packagings (171.8)

Throughout the regulations, packaging requirements are separated according to the two general types of packagings - non-bulk and bulk.

Non-bulk packagings (171.8)

Non-bulk packagings are those having:

- A maximum capacity of 450 L (119 gal) or less, as a receptacle for a liquid,

- A maximum net mass of 400 kg (882 lbs) or less and a maximum capacity of 450 L (119 gal) or less, as a receptacle for a solid, or

- A water capacity of 454 kg (1,000 lbs) or less, as a receptacle for a gas.

Bulk packagings (171.8)

Bulk packagings are those, other than vessels or barges, and including transport vehicles or freight containers, in which hazmat is loaded with no intermediate form of containment and having:

- A maximum capacity greater than 450 L (119 gal) as a receptacle for a liquid,

- A maximum net mass greater than 400 kg (882 lbs) and a maximum capacity greater than 450 L (119 gal), as a receptacle for a solid, or

- A water capacity greater than 454 kg (1,000 lbs), as a receptacle for a gas.

Packaging codes (178.502)

Throughout the regulations, and particularly in Part 173, non-bulk performance-oriented packagings are indicated by codes — such as "1A1" or "6HG1." Codes that contain only one capital letter indicate single packagings, and can be deciphered as follows:

The first numeral designates the type of packaging:

1 = Drum

2 = Wooden barrel

3 = Jerrican

4 = Box

5 = Bag

6 = Composite packaging

7 = Pressure receptacle

The letter indicates the material of construction:

A = Steel (all types and surface treatments)

B = Aluminum

C = Natural wood

D = Plywood

F = Reconstituted wood

Packaging

G = Fiberboard

H = Plastic

L = Textile

M = Paper, multi-wall

N = Metal (other than steel and aluminum)

P = Glass, porcelain, or stoneware

A second numeral indicates the category of packaging within the packaging:

1 = Non-removable head (for drums)

2 = Removable head (for drums)

Example: *"1A1" indicates a steel drum with a non-removable head, while "4D" indicates a plywood box. Codes that contain two capital letters indicate composite packagings. The first letter designates the material for the inner receptacle, and the second, the material for the outer packaging.*

Example: *"6HA1" would be a plastic receptacle in a steel drum with a non-removable head.*

Manufacturers' markings (178.503)

To be acceptable for transport, non-bulk packagings that have to conform to a UN standard must be marked with a manufacturer's marking. The marking must be durable, clearly visible, and include the following:

- United Nations symbol

- Appropriate packaging ID code (such as "1A2") designating:

  - The type of packaging (1 = drum).

  - The material of construction (A = steel).

  - The category of packaging within the packaging (2 = removable head).

- A letter identifying the performance standard under which the packaging design has been sucessfully tested.

Letter	Meaning
X	Packaging meets packing group I, II, and III tests.
Y	Packaging meets packing group II and III tests.
Z	Packaging meets packing group III tests.

- For outer packagings intended to contain liquids — a designation of the specific gravity. (This designation can be omitted if less than 1.2.)

- For inner packagings or packagings intended to contain solids — the maximum gross mass in kilograms.

- For single and composite packagings intended to contain liquids — the test pressure in kilopascals, rounded down to the nearest 10 kPa of hydrostatic pressure that the package has successfully passed.

- For solids and inner packagings — the letter "S."

- The last two digits of the year of manufacture.

- For plastic drums (1H) and jerricans (3H) — the last two digits of the year of manufacture and the month of manufacture.

- The letters "USA" to indicate that the package was manufactured in the USA and marked according to the Hazardous Materials Regulations.

Packaging

- The name and address, or symbol, of the manufacturer or approval agency certifying compliance. Symbols, if used, must be registered with the Associate Administrator for Hazardous Materials Safety.

- The minimum thickness in millimeters (mm) of the packaging materials for metal or plastic drums or jerricans intended for reuse or reconditioning, or of the outer packaging of a composite packaging intended for reuse or reconditioning.

A packaging that has been reconditioned must also be marked — near the previously described markings — with:

- The name of the country in which the reconditioning was performed. In the United States, "USA" is used.

- The name and address, or symbol, of the reconditioner. Symbols, if used, must be registered with the Associate Administrator for Hazardous Materials Safety.

- The last two digits of the year of reconditioning.

- The letter "R" (for reconditioned).

- The letter "L" for packagings that successfully pass the leakproofness test.

Example: *The following marking indicates a fiberboard box (4G) — tested for packing groups II and III (Y) and that has a maximum mass of 145 kg — is designed to contain an inner packaging (S) — was manufactured in 2003 (03) in the United States (USA) by a manufacturer whose registered symbol is (RA).*

4G/Y145/S/03
USA/RA

Example: *The following marking indicates a steel, non-removable head drum (1A1) that has been designed as a single packaging for liquids, tested* *for packing groups II and III (Y), with a specific gravity up to 1.4, and hydrostatically tested to 150 kPa. The drum was manufactured in 2003 (03) in the United States (USA) by a manufacturer whose registered symbol is "VL824." The minimum thickness of the material is 1 millimeter.*

1A1/Y1.4/150/03

USA/VL824

1.0

Example: *The following marking indicates a steel, non-removable head drum (1A1), designed as a single packaging for liquids, tested for packing groups II and III (Y), for materials with a specific gravity of 1.4. It was hydrostatically tested to 150 kPa and was manufactured in 2002 (02). The drum was reconditioned in the United States (USA) by a reconditioner whose registered symbol is "RB" in 2003 (03). The drum was reconditioned (R) and successfully passed the leakproofness test (L).*

1A1/Y1.4/150/02

USA/RB/03 RL

Hazardous Materials Table (172.101)

The Hazardous Materials Table is the starting point for determining the appropriate packaging for a hazardous material. It lists codes for applicable special provisions (Column 7), packaging exceptions (Column 8A), authorized non-bulk packagings (Column 8B), and authorized bulk packagings (Column 8C).

Sample from the Hazardous Materials Table

Symbols	Hazardous materials descriptions and proper shipping names	Hazard class or Division	Identification Numbers	PG	Label Codes	Special provisions (§172.102)	(8) Packaging (§173.***)		
							Exceptions	Nonbulk	Bulk
(1)	(2)	(3)	(4)	(5)	(6)	(7)	(8A)	(8B)	(8C)
	Trichlorobutene	6.1	UN2322	II	6.1	IB2, T7, TP2	153	202	243
	1,1,1-Trichloroethane	6.1	UN2831	III	6.1	IB3, N36, T4, TP1	153	203	241

Example: *In Column 8 of the Hazardous Materials Table, separate packaging authorization codes are listed for non-bulk packagings (8B) and bulk packagings (8C).*

Special provisions (172.102)

Section 172.102 defines the special provision codes listed in Column 7 of the Hazardous Materials Table. The applicability of the provisions for a given material will vary, depending on the quantity being transported and the mode of transport being used. However, many of the special provisions apply to packaging.

Packaging selection

Packaging selection is a multi-step procedure that involves referencing numerous parts of the regulations. Shown below is the procedure that is used to select packagings for materials in Classes 2 through 6, 8, and 9. Information on the proper selection procedures for Classes 1 and 7 can be found in the regulations in Part 173, Subparts C and I, respectively.

Packaging selection for Class 2-6, 8 & 9 materials

To select an appropriate packaging for a material in one of these classes:

✓ Locate the material's proper shipping name, hazard class, and packing group (if any) in the Hazardous Materials Table. If more than one packing group is shown, select the correct one according to the criteria detailed in Subpart D of Part 173.

✓ Review the special provisions listed for the material in Column 7 to determine if any apply. These codes are defined in 172.102.

✓ Review the exceptions listed in Column 8A to determine if any apply. These exceptions are detailed in Part 173.

✓ Refer to either Column 8B (non-bulk) or 8C (bulk), to locate the appropriate section in Part 173 where the authorized packagings will be listed.

✓ Select an appropriate packaging from the lists in Part 173 by taking into consideration the following:

- Material's quantity.

- Material's compatibility with the packaging.

- Mode of transport being used.

✓ Locate the applicable specifications and test standards for the selected packaging in Part 178 or Part 179.

✓ Refer to 173.24 and 173.24a or 173.24b to ensure that the packaging meets the general requirements listed for all packagings and for non-bulk or bulk packagings, as applicable.

Example: *To determine the appropriate packaging for "Acetylene, dissolved," you must first locate the proper shipping name in Column 2 of the Hazardous Materials Table. Looking across the table, you will see that it is a Division 2.1 material which has no packing group and no special provisions.*

Sample from the Hazardous Materials Table

Symbols	Hazardous materials descriptions and proper shipping names	Hazard class or Division	Identification Numbers	PG	Label Codes	Special provisions (§172.102)	(8) Packaging (§173.***)		
							Exceptions	Nonbulk	Bulk
(1)	(2)	(3)	(4)	(5)	(6)	(7)	(8A)	(8B)	(8C)
	Acetylene, dissolved	2.1	UN1001		2.1		None	303	None

Column 8B lists the non-bulk packaging reference "303" — which refers to 173.303, the section where the authorized packagings are listed. For "Acetylene, dissolved," either a Specification 8 or 8AL cylinder would be acceptable.

Packaging exceptions

All packagings of hazmat must be as specified in Part 173, unless exceptions are authorized. The three most common exceptions are:

Small quantities (173.4)

Small quantities of Class 3, Division 4.1, Division 5.1, Division 5.2, Class 8, Division 6.1, Class 9, and Class 7 materials are excepted from the packaging regulations to the extent allowed in 173.4.

Limited quantities (Part 173)

Certain limited quantities of hazardous materials are excepted from the packaging regulations. The exceptions are found in 173.150 for Class 3, 173.151 for Division 4.1, 173.152 for Class 5, 173.153 for Division 6.1, 173.154 for Class 8, 173.155 for Class 9, and 173.306 for Class 2.

Salvage drums (173.3)

Packages of hazardous materials that are damaged, defective, or found leaking, along with hazardous materials that have spilled or leaked, may be placed in a salvage drum for transport to be repackaged or for disposal. Salvage drums are excepted from the packaging regulations to the extent allowed in 173.3(c).

Notes

Notes

Definitions
(171.8)

This is an alphabetical listing of many of the terms commonly used in the hazmat transportation process. For a complete listing, refer to 49 CFR 171.8 Definitions and abbreviations.

Bulk packaging means a packaging, other than a vessel or a barge, including a transport vehicle or freight container, in which hazardous materials are loaded with no intermediate form of containment and that has:

- a maximum capacity greater than 450 L (119 gallons) as a receptacle for a liquid;

- a maximum net mass greater than 400 kg (882 pounds) and a maximum capacity greater than 450 L (119 gallons) as a receptacle for a solid; or

- a water capacity greater than 454 kg (1000 pounds) as a receptacle for a gas as defined in §173.115 of the HMR.

Cargo tank means a bulk packaging that:

- is a tank intended primarily for the carriage of liquids or gases and includes appurtenances, reinforcements, fittings, and closures;

- is permanently attached to or forms a part of a motor vehicle, or is not permanently attached to a motor vehicle but which, by reason of its size, construction or attachment to a motor vehicle is loaded or unloaded without being removed from the motor vehicle; and

- is not fabricated under a specification for cylinders, intermediate bulk containers, multi-unit tank car tanks, portable tanks, or tank cars.

Cargo tank motor vehicle means a motor vehicle with one or more cargo tanks permanently attached to or forming an integral part of the motor vehicle.

Definitions

Carrier means a person who transports passengers or property in commerce by rail car, aircraft, motor vehicle, or vessel.

Class means hazard class. See **Hazard class**.

Consignee means the person or place shown on a shipping document, package marking, or other media as the location to which a carrier is directed to transport a hazardous material.

Consumer commodity means a material that is packaged and distributed in a form intended or suitable for sale through retail sales agencies or instrumentalities for consumption by individuals for purposes of personal care or household use. The term also includes drugs and medicines.

Division means a subdivision of a hazard class.

DOT means U.S. Department of Transportation.

Elevated temperature material means a material which, when offered for transportation or transported in a bulk packaging:

- is in a liquid phase and at a temperature at or above 100 degrees C (212 degrees F);

- is in a liquid phase with a flash point at or above 37.8 degrees C (100 degrees F) that is intentionally heated and offered for transportation or transported at or above its flash point; or

- is in a solid phase and at a temperature at or above 240 degrees C (464 degrees F).

Freight container means a reusable container having a volume of 64 cubic feet or more designed and constructed to permit being lifted with its contents intact and intended primarily for containment of packages during transportation.

Gross weight or **Gross mass** means the weight of a packaging plus the weight of its contents.

Hazard class means the category of hazard assigned to a hazardous material. A material may meet the defining criteria for more than one hazard class, but is assigned to only one hazard class.

Hazard zone means one of four levels of hazard (Hazard Zones A through D) assigned to gases, and one of two levels of hazards (Hazard Zones A and B) assigned to liquids that are poisonous by inhalation.

Hazardous material means a substance or material that the Secretary of Transportation has determined is capable of posing an unreasonable risk to health, safety, and property when transported in commerce, and has designated as hazardous under Section 5103 of federal hazardous materials transportation law. The term includes hazardous substances, hazardous wastes, marine pollutants, elevated temperature materials, materials designated as hazardous in the Hazardous Materials Table, and materials that meet the defining criteria for hazard classes and divisions.

Hazardous waste means any material that is subject to the Hazardous Waste Manifest Requirements of the U.S. Environmental Protection Agency specified in 40 CFR Part 262.

Hazmat employee means:

- A person who is:

    - Employed on a full-time, part time, or temporary basis by a hazmat employer and who in the course of such full time, part time or temporary employment directly affects hazardous materials transportation safety;

    - Self-employed (including an owner-operator of a motor vehicle, vessel, or aircraft) transporting hazardous materials in commerce who in the course of such self-employment directly affects hazardous materials transportation safety;

    - A railroad signalman; or

    - A railroad maintenance-of-way employee.

Definitions

- This term includes an individual, employed on a full time, part time, or temporary basis by a hazmat employer, or who is self-employed, who during the course of employment:

  - Loads, unloads, or handles hazardous materials;

  - Designs, manufactures, fabricates, inspects, marks, maintains, reconditions, repairs, or tests a package, container or packaging component that is represented, marked, certified, or sold as qualified for use in transporting hazardous material in commerce.

  - Prepares hazardous materials for transportation;

  - Is responsible for safety of transporting hazardous materials;

  - Operates a vehicle used to transport hazardous materials.

Hazmat employer means:

- A person who employs or uses at least one hazmat employee on a full-time, part time, or temporary basis; and who:

  - Transports hazardous materials in commerce;

  - Causes hazardous materials to be transported in commerce; or

  - Designs, manufactures, fabricates, inspects, marks, maintains, reconditions, repairs or tests a package, container, or packaging component that is represented, marked, certified, or sold by that person as qualified for use in transporting hazardous materials in commerce;

- A person who is self-employed (including an owner-operator of a motor vehicle, vessel, or aircraft) transporting materials in commerce; and who:

    - Transports hazardous materials in commerce;

    - Causes hazardous materials to be transported in commerce; or

    - Designs, manufactures, fabricates, inspects, marks, maintains, reconditions, repairs or tests a package, container, or packaging component that is represented, marked, certified, or sold by that person as qualified for use in transporting hazardous materials in commerce; or

- A department, agency, or instrumentality of the United States Government, or an authority of a State, political subdivision of a State, or an Indian tribe; and who:

    - Transports hazardous materials in commerce;

    - Causes hazardous materials to be transported in commerce; or

    - Designs, manufactures, fabricates, inspects, marks, maintains, reconditions, repairs or tests a package, container, or packaging component that is represented, marked, certified, or sold by that person as qualified for use in transporting hazardous materials in commerce.

HMR means Hazardous Materials Regulations.

Limited quantity means the maximum amount of a hazardous material for which there is a specific labeling or packaging exception.

Marine pollutant means a material which is listed in Appendix B to §172.101 of the HMR and, when in a solution or mixture of one or more marine pollutants, is packaged in a concentration which equals or exceeds:

- ten percent by weight of the solution or mixture for materials listed in the appendix; or

Definitions

- one percent by weight of the solution or mixture for materials that are identified as severe marine pollutants in the appendix.

Material of trade means a hazardous material, other than a hazardous waste, that is carried on a motor vehicle—

- For the purpose of protecting the health and safety of the motor vehicle operator or passengers;

- For the purpose of supporting the operation or maintenance of a motor vehicle (including its auxiliary equipment); or

- By a private motor carrier (including vehicles operated by a rail carrier) in direct support of a principal business that is other than transportation by motor vehicle.

Material poisonous by inhalation means:

- a gas meeting the defining criteria in §173.115(c) of the HMR and assigned to Hazard Zone A, B, C, or D in accordance with §173.116(a) of the HMR;

- a liquid (other than as a mist) meeting the defining criteria in §173.132(a)(1)(iii) of the HMR, and assigned to Hazard Zone A or B in accordance with §173.133(a) of the HMR; or

- any material identified as an inhalation hazard by a special provision in Column 7 of the §172.101 Table of the HMR.

Mode means any of the following transportation methods; rail, highway, air, or water.

Motor vehicle includes a vehicle, machine, tractor, trailer or semi-trailer, or any combination thereof, propelled or drawn by mechanical power and used upon the highways in the transportation of passengers or property. It does not include a vehicle, locomotive, or car operated exclusively on a rail or rails, or a trolley bus operated by electric power derived from a fixed overhead wire, furnishing local passenger transportation similar to street/railway service.

NA means North American.

Non-bulk packaging means a packaging which has:

- a maximum capacity of 450 L (119 gallons) or less as a receptacle for a liquid;

- a maximum net mass of 400 kg (882 pounds) or less and a maximum capacity of 450 L (119 gallons) or less as a receptacle for a solid; or

- a water capacity of 454 kg (1000 pounds) or less as a receptacle for a gas as defined in §173.115 of the HMR.

N.O.S. means not otherwise specified.

ORM means other regulated material.

Overpack means an enclosure that is used by a single consignor to provide protection or convenience in handling of a package or to consolidate two or more packages. Overpack does not include a transport vehicle, freight container, or aircraft unit load device. Examples of overpacks are one or more packages:

- placed or stacked onto a load board such as a pallet and secured by strapping, shrink wrapping, stretch wrapping, or other suitable means; or

- placed in a protective outer packaging such as a box or crate.

Packaging means a receptacle and any other components or materials necessary for the receptacle to perform its containment function in conformance with the minimum packing requirements of the HMR.

Packing group means a grouping according to the degree of danger presented by hazardous materials. Packing Group I indicates great danger; Packing Group II, medium danger; Packing Group III, minor danger.

Person means an individual, corporation, company, association, firm, partnership, society, joint stock company; or a government, Indian tribe, or authority of a government or tribe offering a hazardous material for transportation in commerce or transporting a hazardous material to support a commercial enterprise. This term does not include the United States Postal

Definitions

Service or, for purposes of 49 U.S.C. 5123 and 5124, a Department, agency, or instrumentality of the government.

Person who offers or **offeror** means:

- Any person who does either or both of the following:

  - Performs, or is responsible for performing, any pre-transportation function required under this subchapter for transportation of the hazardous material in commerce.

  - Tenders or makes the hazardous material available to a carrier for transportation in commerce.

- A carrier is not an offeror when it performs a function required by this subchapter as a condition of acceptance of a hazardous material for transportation in commerce (e.g., reviewing shipping papers, examining packages to ensure that they are in conformance with this subchapter, or preparing shipping documentation for its own use) or when it transfers a hazardous material to another carrier for continued transportation in commerce without performing a pre-transportation function.

PHMSA means the Pipeline and Hazardous Materials Safety Administration, U.S. Department of Transportation, Washington, DC 20590.

Primary hazard means the hazard class of a material as assigned in the §172.101 Table of the HMR.

Proper shipping name means the name of the hazardous material shown in Roman print (not italics) in §172.101 of the HMR.

Reportable quantity (RQ) means the quantity specified in Column 2 of the Appendix to §172.101 of the HMR, for any material identified in Column 1 of the Appendix.

Residue means the hazardous material remaining in a packaging, including a tank car, after its contents have been unloaded to the maximum extent practicable and before the packaging is either refilled or cleaned of hazardous materials and purged to remove any hazardous vapors.

Shipping paper means a shipping order, bill of lading, manifest or other shipping document serving a similar purpose and containing the information required by §172.202, §172.203 and §172.204 of the HMR.

Special permit means a document issued by the Associate Administrator under the authority of 49 U.S.C. 5117 permitting a person to perform a function that is not otherwise permitted under subchapter A or C of this chapter, or other regulations issued under 49 U.S.C. 5101 et seq. (e.g., Federal Motor Carrier Safety routing requirements). The terms "special permit" and "exemption" have the same meaning for purposes of subchapter A or C of this chapter or other regulations issued under 49 U.S.C. 5101 through 5127. An exemption issued prior to October 1, 2005 remains valid until it is past its expiration date, terminated by the Associate Administrator, or issued as a special permit, whichever occurs first.

Specification packaging means a packaging conforming to one of the specifications or standards for packagings in Part 178 or 179 of the HMR.

Subsidiary hazard means a hazard of a material other than the primary hazard. See **Primary hazard**.

Technical name means a recognized chemical name or microbiological name currently used in scientific and technical handbooks, journals, and texts. Generic descriptions are authorized for use as technical names provided they readily identify the general chemical group, or microbiological group. Except for names which appear in Subpart B of Part 172 of the HMR, trade names may not be used as technical names.

Transport vehicle means a cargo-carrying vehicle such as an automobile, van, tractor, truck, semitrailer, tank car or rail car used for the transportation of cargo by any mode. Each cargo-carrying body (trailer, rail car, etc.) is a separate transport vehicle.

UN means United Nations.

UN standard packaging means a packaging conforming to standards in the UN Recommendations.

Unit load device means any type of freight container, aircraft container, aircraft pallet with a net, or aircraft pallet with a net over an igloo.

Notes

Name:_____

Date:_____

Hazmat Made Easier Quiz

1. **What is the first challenge a hazmat employee must face in the hazmat transportation process?**
   a. Determining whether a material is hazardous.
   b. Determining how to ship a material.
   c. Determining whether placards will be needed.
   d. Determining whether shipping papers will be needed.

2. **What is the most important step in using the Hazardous Materials Table?**
   a. Making sure the Table you are using is up-to-date.
   b. Choosing the correct proper shipping name.
   c. Choosing the correct packing group (PG) for the material you are shipping.
   d. Choosing the correct placard (s) for the material you are shipping.

3. **How many symbols are used to identify hazmat with special shipping instructions in Column 1 of the Hazardous Materials Table?**
   a. Four
   b. Five
   c. Six
   d. Seven

4. **PG numbers are not assigned to**
   a. Class 2 materials.
   b. Class 7 materials.
   c. ORM-D materials.
   d. All of the above.

5. **Hazmat entries on a shipping paper must**
   a. Be entered first.
   b. Identified with an "X" or "RQ", in a column designated "HM."
   c. Entered in a contrasting color.
   d. All of the above.

Notes